HORRIBLE JOBS IN

COLONIAL TIMES

Gareth Stevens
Publishing

LOUISE
SPILSBURY

Please visit our website, www.garethstevens.com.
For a free color catalog of all our high-quality books,
call toll free 1-800-542-2595 or fax 1-877-542-2596.

Library of Congress Cataloging-in-Publication Data

Spilsbury, Louise.
Horrible jobs in colonial times / by Louise Spilsbury.
  p. cm. — (History's most horrible jobs)
Includes index.
ISBN 978-1-4824-0331-2 (pbk.)
ISBN 978-1-4824-0333-6 (6-pack)
ISBN 978-1-4824-0330-5 (library binding)
1. Handicraft — United States — History — 17th century — Juvenile literature. 2. Artisans —
United States — History — Juvenile literature. 3. United States – Social life and customs — To
1775 — Juvenile literature. I. Spilsbury, Louise. II. Title.
E162.S65 2014
973.3—dc23

First Edition

Published in 2014 by
Gareth Stevens Publishing
111 East 14th Street, Suite 349
New York, NY 10003

© 2014 Gareth Stevens Publishing

Produced by Calcium, www.calciumcreative.co.uk
Designed by Simon Borrough
Edited by Sarah Eason and Rachel Blount

Cover Illustration by Jim Mitchell

Photo credits: Dreamstime: Americanspirit 4, 20, Andykazie 14, Barbndave 25, Eg004713
39, Gary718 6, Kenneystudios 27, Leesniderphotoimages 15, 23, 38, Missouriphotos 16,
Vgoodrich 36; Duke University Libraries: 13; Getty Images: Hulton Archive 8; Shutterstock:
Anneka 37, Yulia Avgust 34, Balefire 21b, Jorge Felix Costa 33, Ermess 18b, Donald Gargano
7, Mark Grenier 42, Intoit 45, Eric Isselee 18t, Joppo 35l, Robert Kyllo 35r, Paul Maguire 40l,
Makar 17l, MarcelClemens 43b, Tom Mc Nemar 30, N4 PhotoVideo 44, Nattika 24, NeonLight
10, An Nguyen 12, Zavodskov Anatoliy Nikolaevich 26b, Ola-ola 22b, Tom Oliveira 29, Olga
Popova 32, Projektograf 9, R. Gino Santa Maria 26t, RedDaxLuma 17r, Luba Shushpanova 43t,
Rechitan Sorin 31, Spirit of America 11, Sydeen 41, Diana Taliun 40r, Travel Bug 21t, 22t, Rudy
Umans 28; Wikimedia Commons: Robert Walter Weir, Google Art project 5.

Printed in the United States of America.

CPSIA compliance information: Batch #CW14GS: For further information contact Gareth Stevens, New York, New York at 1-800-542-2595.

Contents

Chapter One
Life in Colonial Times

From the early 1500s, waves of people from Europe started to arrive on the shores of the Americas. Among the first Europeans to explore what is now the United States were the Spanish. In 1607, English settlers founded their first colony at Jamestown, Virginia. By 1733, there were 13 English colonies along the Atlantic Coast. Why did so many people want to settle here?

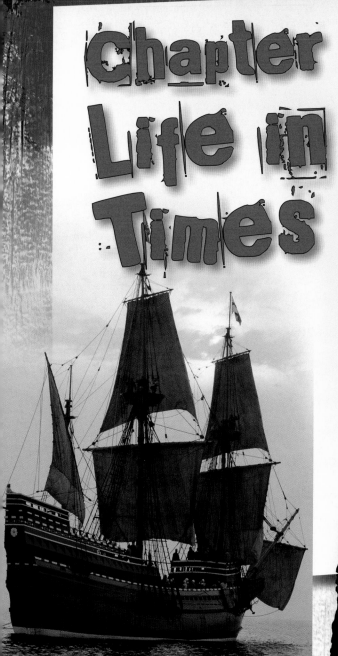

This is the *Mayflower II*. It is a replica of the original ship *Mayflower*, which carried the Pilgrims to Plymouth, Massachusetts, in 1620.

Land of Hope and Glory

Some people traveled to North America for adventure and opportunities. They had heard tales of the wide expanses of land that families could claim for farms. Some came to find a place where they could follow their religion freely, which they had been unable to do in their home countries. The Pilgrims, founders of Plymouth, Massachusetts, arrived in 1620. They barely survived their first winter even with help and food from nearby Native American tribes.

A Tough Start

When the first colonists arrived in North America, they discovered a land quite different from the one they had left behind. It was empty, wild, and untamed. Nine out of 10 of the early colonists were farmers. They had to build their own homes and grow or hunt for their food. They grew corn and wheat, and raised chickens, sheep, and cattle. They worked incredibly hard, for long hours. Even as the colonies became successful, there were still many horrible jobs to do!

Pilgrims traveled to America to practice their religious beliefs. By 1621, half of those who sailed on the *Mayflower* had died.

Slave Labor

In the southern colonies, huge farms became plantations where colonists grew tobacco and other crops that they exported to England. These huge plantations soon required an army of workers, so slaves were brought in. By the early 1700s, enslaved Africans made up a growing percentage of the colonial population.

Farmwork

In colonial times there were no tractors, combine harvesters, or mechanized plows. Farmers could not use machines to help them do their work. They had to do everything themselves, or with the help of tools they made from the materials they found around them.

Child Labor

Compared with life today, being a child in colonial times was horrible. There was a lot of work to do on a farm, and laziness was considered a sin, so children started carrying out chores from as young as 5 years old. Boys worked with their fathers in the fields, while girls helped their mothers with household chores and meals.

Farmers cut down trees and used the wood to build their homes and barns.

Colonists worked hard for many hours a day, and most days of the week. However, despite their heavy workload, they always went to church. People who failed to attend church at least once a month were fined or punished!

Farmer's Wife

The job of a farmer's wife was truly horrible! Along with caring for the children, she worked in the family garden and preserved the vegetables she grew for winter. She milked cows and made butter and cheese. She made soaps and candles, spun yarn from wool, sewed, fixed, and washed clothes and linen, cooked the meals, and cleaned the house. A farmer's wife didn't stop from dawn until dusk!

In colonial times, a farmer's wife had to do all her jobs by hand. By the eighteenth century, spinning wheels, butter churns, and equipment for making cheese had been invented, making women's lives easier.

Indentured Servants

Running a colonial farm was hard work. However, plantations were huge and required many workers. Plantation owners found it difficult to hire workers already in the colonies—most colonials wanted to own their own plantation, not work on one. As a result, plantation owners hired indentured servants.

Passage Paid

Indentured servants were young workers in Europe whom the plantation owners paid to travel to America. The workers then owed the plantation owner their travel fares, and had to work on the plantation for several years to pay off the debts. Indentured servants were mainly young men between the ages of 15 and 25 years.

Up to three-quarters of the people who settled in North America in the seventeenth century were indentured servants.

A Life of Labor

The life of an indentured servant was truly horrible. He worked incredibly hard on the land, digging, planting, weeding, and tending plants, but received no wages for 7 years. The servant's master provided food and lodgings, but these were often very poor. To make matters worse, a servant was often beaten by his master. Some servants were even beaten to death.

Tobacco from America's native tobacco plant was the most valuable export from the colonies between 1617 and 1793.

Backbreaking Work

It has been estimated that an indentured servant working 4 acres (1.6 ha) of corn and tending 1,000 tobacco plants in colonial America would bend over at least 50,000 times!

Field Workers

From around 1620, African slaves were brought to North America. At first, most were treated as indentured servants who could earn their freedom. However, by the 1660s, more and more were brought in chains to work on rice, tobacco, and cotton plantations without the promise of freedom.

Plantation owners grew very rich by using indentured servants and slaves. They built grand homes to show off their wealth.

The Longest Days

Being a field slave was truly horrible. A field slave worked during every hour of daylight. During harvest, they often worked in the fields for 15 to 18 hours a day. Slaves did not usually work on Sundays. Field slaves raked fields, burned stubble, and dug ground before planting. Then they picked the crops. On rice plantations, they also had to flood, drain, dry, hoe, and weed fields before the harvest.

THE HORRIBLE TRUTH

On a cotton plantation, slaves had to pick a certain amount of cotton every day. A white male overseer was paid by the master to make sure the slaves never slowed down. If they did, the overseer whipped the slaves.

Female field workers had to work the same hours as men. Women who were pregnant worked until their babies were born. Then they had to return to work immediately, carrying the babies on their backs. Field workers lived in tiny huts with dirt floors. They were given little food. Slaves slept on makeshift beds, under rough blankets. It was a truly horrible life.

Slaves were subjected to long hours of horrible work and violence from often cruel masters.

Indigo Growers

During colonial times, all blue fabrics were dyed with natural indigo, made from leaves of the indigo plant. Plantation owners shipped and sold the dye to England, where it was used to color cloth. Many European military uniforms used blue cloth at that time, so there was a great demand for indigo.

Blue Indigo

Both male and female slaves worked in the fields, planting and cutting indigo in the hot sun. After harvest, an even more horrible job began. Once cut, indigo plants were loaded on wagons and carried to processing plants. There, workers had to stir, beat, boil, and bubble the weed in huge vats of water and chemicals, while the weed fermented.

Leaves of the indigo plant were the main source of natural indigo.

A Deadly Job

Fermenting indigo gave off dangerous fumes. The plant was often infested with disease-carrying insects, too. Long-term exposure to the plant and its fumes when fermenting harmed the health of workers. The working life span for slaves who made indigo was just 5 to 7 years.

Fighting the Fumes

The fumes and foul stench from fermenting vats were almost unbearable, so the vats were always located far from where most people lived. When the indigo plants had fully rotted, workers drained them of water. The remaining sludge was put in the sun to dry into squares called bricks. Workers had to fan away the flies that gathered around the stinky sludge. If flies laid eggs in the bricks, the maggots that later hatched would make the bricks rot.

Flies attracted by the foul smell from an indigo processing plant spread illness among workers.

Chapter Two
Country
Craftspeople

Early colonists were self-sufficient. They cut down trees to build their own homes, and caught and grew enough food for themselves and their families. Gradually, as colonies grew and more everyday items were needed, household industries developed. People set up businesses that suited their own particular skills.

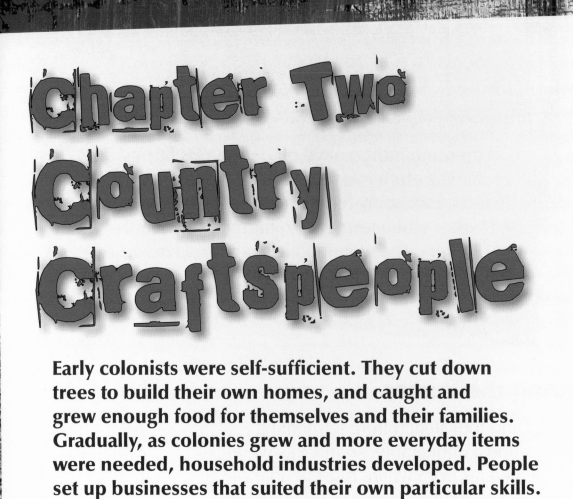

As colonies grew, villages and towns developed new industries to supply people's needs.

A carpenter's main job was to cut and join timber to build colonial wooden homes and stores.

Village Industries

Farms consisting of a house, barn, yard, and fields were usually clustered around villages. In the village, craftspeople performed their trades to help farmers and other settlers. Carpenters and cabinetmakers made tools for the farm and furniture for homes. Millers ran mills that turned the wheat farmers grew into flour to make bread. Weavers turned the cotton and wool that people harvested into cloth or clothing. Cobblers turned the leather from animal hides into tough shoes and boots for working folk.

Apprentices

Boys went to school until they were about 9. Then they had to work. Some worked with their father; others became an apprentice to a craftsman. This meant leaving home to live, learn, and work in a master's shop for 5 to 7 years without pay. The boys had to obey lots of rules. Some were treated well, but others worked long hours and had to sleep on the workroom floor. Many were treated as servants, too, and had to do household chores before and after a long, hard day's work in their master's shop.

Girl Apprentices

Some girls became apprentices, but really they were little more than indentured servants. Most were not taught a trade. They did household chores for the master and his family—skills that prepared them for marriage, not a career!

BlackSmiths

During colonial times, the Industrial Revolution was in progress in England, and many products were made in factories. In North America, most colonists had to make what they needed by hand. The blacksmith became the most important tradesman in a village, because he made and repaired the iron tools people needed for farming, household tasks, and to carry out other trades.

An Important Job

The blacksmith heated iron and shaped it to make and mend tools. He made hinges, nails, axes, spades, and other tools for tradesmen and farmers. The blacksmith also made kettles, cutlery, pots, and pans for homes. Blacksmiths were well respected, however the job could be dangerous. A blacksmith's workshop, or forge, was attached to his house. The threat that it could catch fire was constant.

If a blacksmith did not contantly watch his fire, it might quickly spread from his forge to his wooden home.

THE HORRIBLE TRUTH

Sometimes a blacksmith acted as a dentist, too! He had a variety of metal tools, such as pliers, for gripping and pulling out blackened and rotten teeth—ouch!

Colonial blacksmiths beat red-hot metal with heavy hammers. It was hot, sweaty, and often dangerous work.

Dangers at Work

A blacksmith created heat to melt iron by burning charcoal in a huge hearth. He blasted it with air from hand bellows, until it was extremely hot. Once the metal was soft, he beat it into shape with a hammer, while resting the metal on a huge anvil. Then he plunged the metal into a large vat of water. This cooled it instantly. Colonial blacksmiths had no gloves to protect them from the tongs they used to hold metal. As a result, they were often burned.

Blacksmiths used tools such as pliers to pull out rotten teeth in colonial times.

Tanners

Many colonists depended on a tanner to convert the raw hides of farm animals such as cattle, pigs, sheep, and goats into leather. People did not have synthetic materials in colonial times, so leather was an important resource. People used leather for clothing, shoes, and many other products.

Leather in Everyday Life

Many men in colonial times wore leather undershirts. Leather was used to make saddles and bridles used by farmers. Soldiers needed leather for boots, saddles, and the sheaths that held their swords. Chairs often had leather seats, and books were bound in leather. Rich people sat on seats made of leather in their fine, lavish coaches.

Tanners made leather from the skins of animals such as goats.

Colonial cobblers relied on tanners for leather to make boots and shoes.

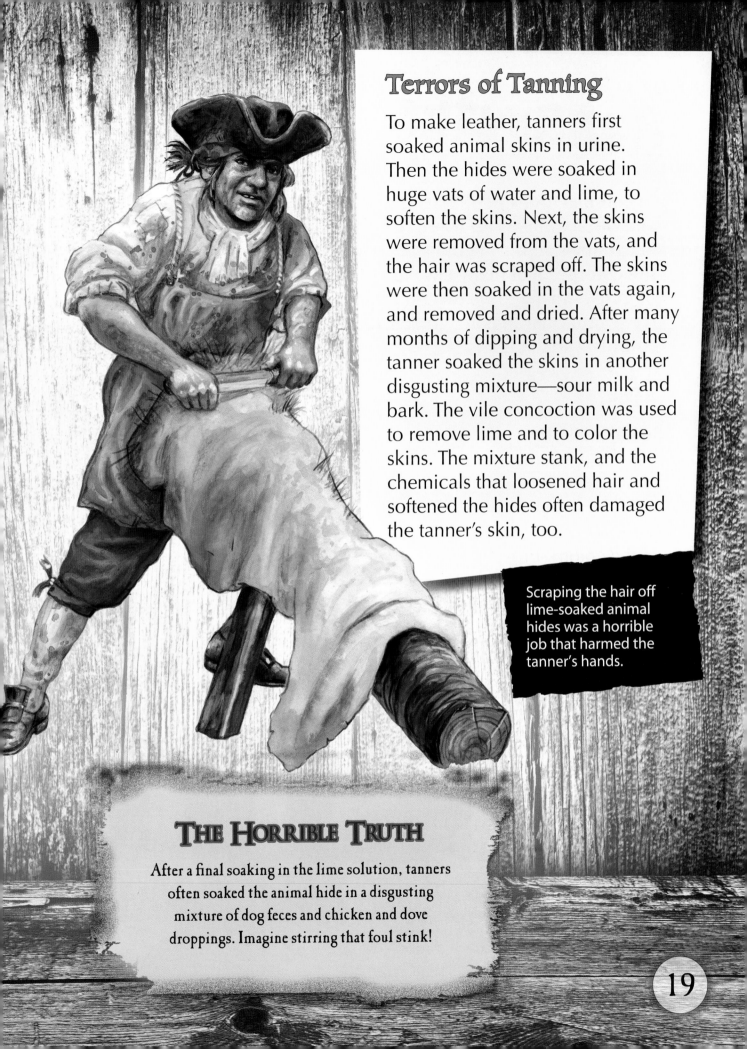

Terrors of Tanning

To make leather, tanners first soaked animal skins in urine. Then the hides were soaked in huge vats of water and lime, to soften the skins. Next, the skins were removed from the vats, and the hair was scraped off. The skins were then soaked in the vats again, and removed and dried. After many months of dipping and drying, the tanner soaked the skins in another disgusting mixture—sour milk and bark. The vile concoction was used to remove lime and to color the skins. The mixture stank, and the chemicals that loosened hair and softened the hides often damaged the tanner's skin, too.

Scraping the hair off lime-soaked animal hides was a horrible job that harmed the tanner's hands.

THE HORRIBLE TRUTH

After a final soaking in the lime solution, tanners often soaked the animal hide in a disgusting mixture of dog feces and chicken and dove droppings. Imagine stirring that foul stink!

Gunsmiths

In colonial times people used guns to hunt deer and other animals for food, for self-defense, and to kill animals so they could sell their skins. Although the colonies had many laws to control the use of guns, most people owned them. Gunsmiths were kept busy making guns for both colonists and soldiers.

Muster

In colonial times, all men between the ages of 16 and 60 were required to maintain a gun for the defense of the colony. In colonies such as Virginia, men also had to serve in the local militia. They had to muster, or assemble, several times each year to practice. Militia units kept the peace, fought Native Americans, and put down slave rebellions in the South.

On muster days, soldiers had to show their officers that they were suitably dressed and armed.

Gunsmiths at Work

A gunsmith's job was horrible because it was so dangerous. Gunsmiths could injure themselves with the tools they used. When they handled and fixed guns, exploding gunpowder often resulted in terrible injuries. Many gunsmiths became deaf because when they tested guns to see if they were working properly, their ears were damaged by the ear-piercing explosions.

Most gunsmiths learned their skills during an apprenticeship.

Flintlock

When the trigger on a colonial flintlock gun was pulled, a metal piece, called a cock, fell and hit a piece of flint. This made the flint strike a piece of steel, creating sparks. The sparks fell into a gunpowder charge and this powder ignited the charge in the gun's barrel. Bang!

Many of the guns in colonial America were flintlocks, like this one.

Wheelwrights

Wheelwrights kept the wheels of colonial life turning. Without them, colonists could not have traveled farther inland and settled there. There were no electric saws or drills in colonial times, so wheelwrights were in high demand.

Wheelwrights had to form wheels in perfect circles.

Colonists On the Move

Wheelwrights made wheels for carriages, wagons, and riding chairs, and for wheelbarrows and carts used to farm the land. They also built and repaired carts and carriages used by mills. A wheelwright had to cut, shape, and join different types of wood together. They made hubs, or the middle of the wheel, the spokes that radiated out from the hub, and the circular rims of the wheels, called felloes.

 Rough Roads

Colonial roads were little more than dirt lanes littered with ruts and rocks. Wheelwrights had to make wheels that were strong enough to withstand these difficult conditions.

Some wheelwrights worked along coaching routes, to repair coach wheels when they stopped for the night.

Red-hot Tires

Most wooden felloes were bound in metal. Metal-binding was hard work. Two wooden wheels were held together while the iron band, called the shoe, was nailed over the seam where they joined. To be able to shape the metal, the shoe had to be red hot. The heat made the wood of the felloe smoke, and often burned the wheelwrights. Buckets of water were kept close by, to sooth singed hands. Cool water was also poured onto the wheel, to make the iron tire shrink and create a tight fit.

23

Millers

In colonial times, most people ate bread. Early colonists made small amounts of flour by crushing grains between stones or by using a mortar and pestle. In later colonial times, they paid the local miller to grind wheat and corn into flour at his mill.

Millstones

All mills had two large, grooved disks of rock called millstones. These turned and crushed grain into flour. Some millers used waterwheels. Waterwheels used moving river water to turn gear wheels, which then spun the top millstone inside the mill. Being a miller was hard work. A miller had to heave huge, heavy sacks of flour and grain around all day long.

In colonial times, most meals included bread.

Moving Mills

Windmills had vanes or sails that turned in the wind. This action turned gears inside the mill that spun the millstones. Some windmills had bases that could rotate. Millers moved the base to point the vanes into the wind. Other windmills had fixed bases. Millers often worked at night or during storms, when the wind was blowing the most. In the dark, they were in constant danger of being hit by the moving vanes of the windmill.

Millers at large mills often bought grain, processed it, and then sold the flour. Flour was exported to England.

Mills On Fire

Fires were a constant threat to millers. If the dry, powdery dust that floated off crushed grains during milling was not swept up quickly, it could build up, explode, and burn the mill.

Chapter Three
Fishing and Trading

Colonists traveled to North America across the sea, so most of the early settlers set up homes, villages, and towns around harbors along the coast. The sea became a source of great wealth for many colonists.

Many people worked in the shipping industry, including blacksmiths, who made anchors, and wheelwrights, who built ships' wheels.

Exports to Europe

In coastal settlements, people caught fish and whales to eat and sell, and used ships for trading. Wooden sailing ships carried tobacco from the southern colonies to England. They carried rice and indigo to Europe from the swamp lands in South Carolina. Building ships was hard work and required many different workers. Loggers chopped down pine trees by hand, using axes. Carpenters and joiners cut, shaped, and joined the wood. Also employed were sail makers, painters, blacksmiths, and caulkers. Caulkers sealed the joints between the planks of wood on a ship, to make it watertight.

Strong Coopers

There were no rubber, metal, or plastic containers during colonial times. It was the job of the cooper to make buckets and barrels from wood to carry and store food and liquids, such as water, milk, flour, and gunpowder. Coopers also made containers to carry other commodities, such as tobacco, which were transported by ship for sale in Europe. On many large ships, a cooper traveled onboard to mend the ship's barrels. The tools used by coopers were heavier than those of many other tradesmen, so coopers had to be very strong.

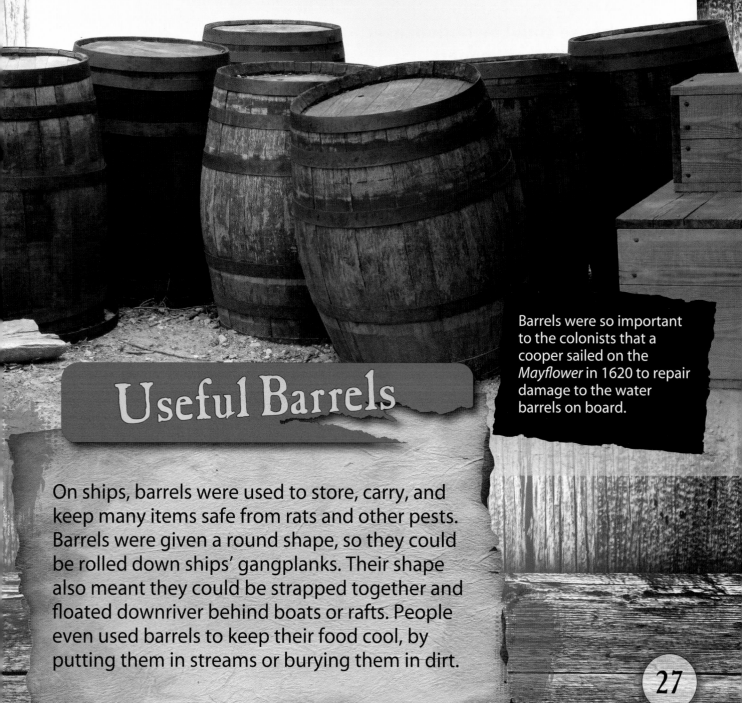

Useful Barrels

Barrels were so important to the colonists that a cooper sailed on the *Mayflower* in 1620 to repair damage to the water barrels on board.

On ships, barrels were used to store, carry, and keep many items safe from rats and other pests. Barrels were given a round shape, so they could be rolled down ships' gangplanks. Their shape also meant they could be strapped together and floated downriver behind boats or rafts. People even used barrels to keep their food cool, by putting them in streams or burying them in dirt.

Lonely Lighthouse Keeper

It was the job of the lighthouse keeper to guide ships safely into harbor with light. Life in a lighthouse could be both dangerous and boring. Many lighthouse keepers spent day after day alone in the lighthouse tower.

Light in the Night

Lighthouses had to be tall buildings so their light could be seen by ships in the distance. During the night, lighthouse keepers had to carry whale oil up the many stairs of a lighthouse tower, to fill the oil lamps at the top. During the night, keepers climbed the stairs three times to check the lamps were burning brightly. They climbed them again, to put out the lamps at sunrise.

Sailors relied on lighthouses to navigate treacherous coastlines.

Lighthouse keepers sometimes had to rescue stranded sailors in small boats.

THE HORRIBLE TRUTH

In 1716, a lighthouse keeper from one of the first lighthouses, on Little Brewster Island in Boston Harbor, drowned along with his wife and daughter. They were in a small boat and couldn't make it to shore because of the rough sea.

On Rough Seas

Lighthouse keepers faced danger along with hard work. They had to climb the tower to clean and paint it, and fix lights. When the weather was too foggy for sailors to see the lamps, keepers shot cannons at timed intervals, to warn ships they were approaching rocks. If a ship got into difficulties, lighthouse keepers set out in small boats to rescue any sailors who were lost at sea.

Tar and Pitch Makers

Pitch and tar were used on ships and were valuable exports. Both products are made from pine trees. Tar is produced by burning pine branches and logs and pitch is produced by boiling tar to concentrate it.

From Sap to Tar

Pine trees contain a sticky substance called sap. Sap leaks from trees through holes or cracks in bark. Shipbuilders spread pitch onto a boat to prevent leaks. Colonists found that sap could also be used to protect other wood. It also stopped ropes and sail rigging from decaying. Colonial ships and the English Navy used tar to fix leaking boats.

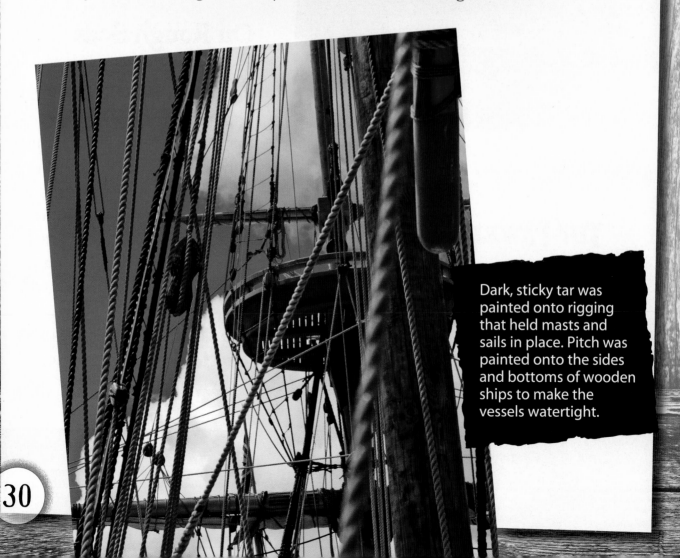

Dark, sticky tar was painted onto rigging that held masts and sails in place. Pitch was painted onto the sides and bottoms of wooden ships to make the vessels watertight.

Pitch and tar are thick and sticky. Making pitch and tar was a horrible, dangerous job.

Making Pitch and Tar

Tar makers cut wood, piled it over a pit, and covered it with earth. They then set the wood alight. After burning for a long time, the wood sap turned to black tar, and dripped into the pit. A gutter carried tar from the pit to a trough. A tar maker tended his fires constantly. It was his job to climb onto the burning pile and seal holes in the dirt, to keep the fires burning slowly. Tar makers were often burned by, or covered in, thick, sticky tar.

Black Heat

When tar was boiled to make pitch, it bubbled ferociously. Just one drop of this sticky substance could burn skin instantly. Tar and pitch makers often worked in forests, so if they were badly burned, there was no hope of any medical help.

Whalers

Colonists soon discovered a use for dead whales that washed up onto the shore. They ate the meat of the dead animal, and used its fat to make oil. From the 1720s, large colonial ships set out to hunt whales in deep waters. Whaling was dangerous, but profitable, work. In colonial times, it soon became big business.

Whale Wares

Whalers brought dead whales to shore, and cut up their blubber and bone. Oil was extracted from the blubber by boiling it in huge iron pots. The colonists ate and sold whale meat, and used whale oil for lamps and soap. They made whale bones into corsets and buttons. A substance called ambergris was also extracted from the carcass and used to make medicine and perfume.

Whales were valuable commodities in colonial times, valued for their meat and rich oil.

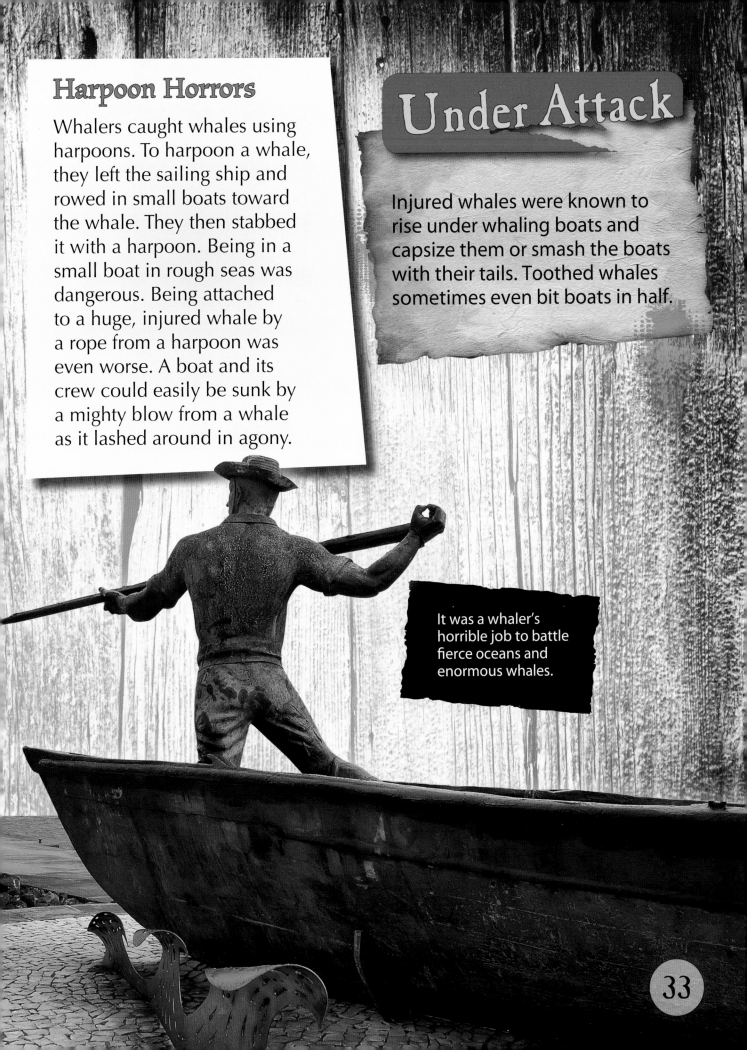

Harpoon Horrors

Whalers caught whales using harpoons. To harpoon a whale, they left the sailing ship and rowed in small boats toward the whale. They then stabbed it with a harpoon. Being in a small boat in rough seas was dangerous. Being attached to a huge, injured whale by a rope from a harpoon was even worse. A boat and its crew could easily be sunk by a mighty blow from a whale as it lashed around in agony.

Under Attack

Injured whales were known to rise under whaling boats and capsize them or smash the boats with their tails. Toothed whales sometimes even bit boats in half.

It was a whaler's horrible job to battle fierce oceans and enormous whales.

Fur Trappers

The colonial fur trade started when fishermen began to trade small items for fur trapped by Native Americans. Gradually, this developed into an important early export. Some colonists were trappers. Others were fur traders who traded with Native American trappers for skins and furs.

Before the colonists came, between 60 and 400 million beavers lived in North America. By the 1900s, this number had dropped to 100,000.

Demand for Fur

In Europe in the seventeenth century, fur coats and felt hats (made from the furry underside of pelts) were highly fashionable. However, Europeans had already killed most of the beavers in Europe. North America became a new source for pelts, and beavers became a valuable commodity for colonists. During the mid-seventeenth century, more than 40,000 pelts a year were sent to England from New York alone.

Trapping Beavers

Trappers stalked beavers with iron-tipped spears and guns, or set traps to catch them. Once the animal was dead, the really horrible part of the job began. Trappers had to travel a long way from the forests, where the animals they trapped lived, to the nearest trading post to sell their catch. The only valuable part of the beaver was its skin, so rather than transport the entire animal, the trapper removed the skin by hand, and left the body behind.

Once removed from the body, an animal's fur was often stretched out to dry, like this.

Fur trappers used traps to catch animals. Iron traps like this one were made by blacksmiths.

Trading Posts

Traders and trappers built trading posts in the wilderness, and settlements grew up around many of these. Some even became major cities, such as Detroit, Michigan; New Orleans, Louisiana; and St. Louis, Missouri.

Chapter Four
Towns and Cities

Many colonists lived in rural areas where there were no nearby towns and where they had to fend for themselves. However, some settlements developed into large, bustling towns. By the 1700s, a large town such as Boston offered people many jobs that smaller settlements could not.

Products could be easily imported and exported across the ocean in colonial times, so the first towns grew up along rivers and coasts.

Urban Life

In colonial towns, tailors, milliners, and hatters made outfits for wealthy people. In some towns, printers printed papers and books, which they supplied to bookstores. The very rich could also hire an architect to design a big house for them to live in. Silversmiths and goldsmiths made and repaired items such as spoons, buttons, and shoe buckles. Music halls provided entertainment, and taverns offered food and a place for people to stay when they were traveling.

Wig Makers

In towns and cities, where there were plenty of wealthy landowners and plantation farmers, the wig maker was always busy. Wig makers made wigs in particular styles for individual customers. They also made wigs that copied the styles of fashionable European wigs. Wig makers were very busy when courts were in session, because judges and attorneys wore unique hairpieces. Being a wig maker was not a pleasant job. Wigs were made from horse, goat, or yak's hair, as well as human hair. Many people had dirty hair or lice-ridden scalps, so styling their hair and fitting wigs to their heads was a pretty horrible job!

A wig maker created wigs on a type of stand called a blockhead.

Blockhead!

Today, people sometimes use the word "blockhead" to mean a fool. The term comes from the name of the wooden models that wig makers used to make their creations.

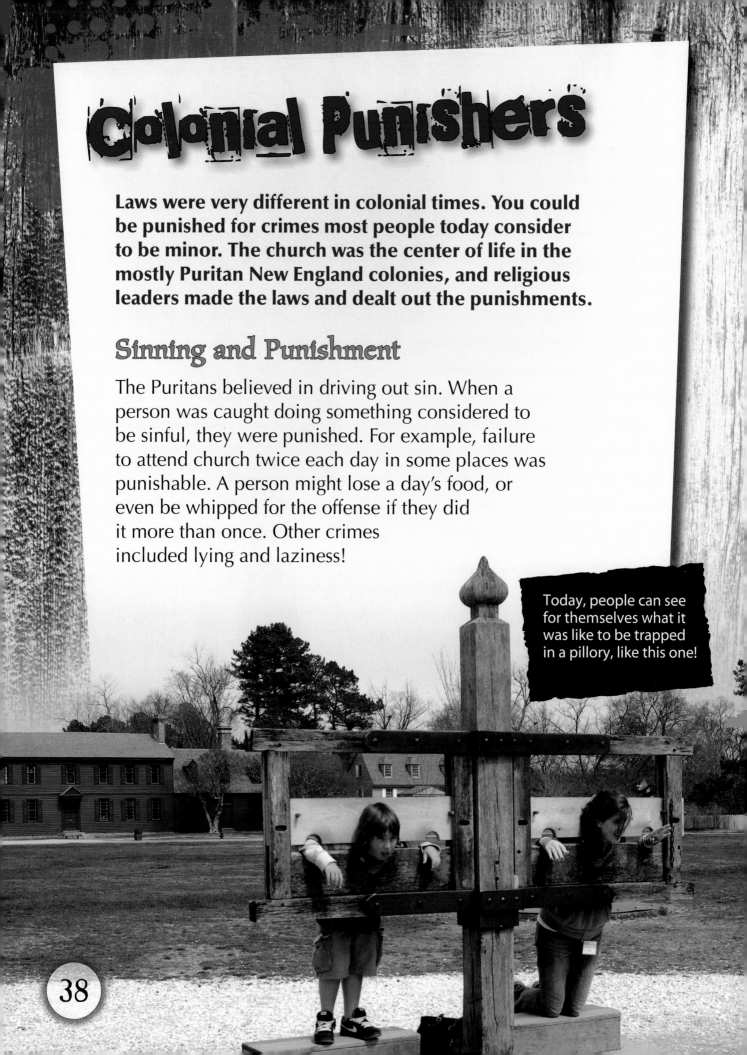

Colonial Punishers

Laws were very different in colonial times. You could be punished for crimes most people today consider to be minor. The church was the center of life in the mostly Puritan New England colonies, and religious leaders made the laws and dealt out the punishments.

Sinning and Punishment

The Puritans believed in driving out sin. When a person was caught doing something considered to be sinful, they were punished. For example, failure to attend church twice each day in some places was punishable. A person might lose a day's food, or even be whipped for the offense if they did it more than once. Other crimes included lying and laziness!

Today, people can see for themselves what it was like to be trapped in a pillory, like this one!

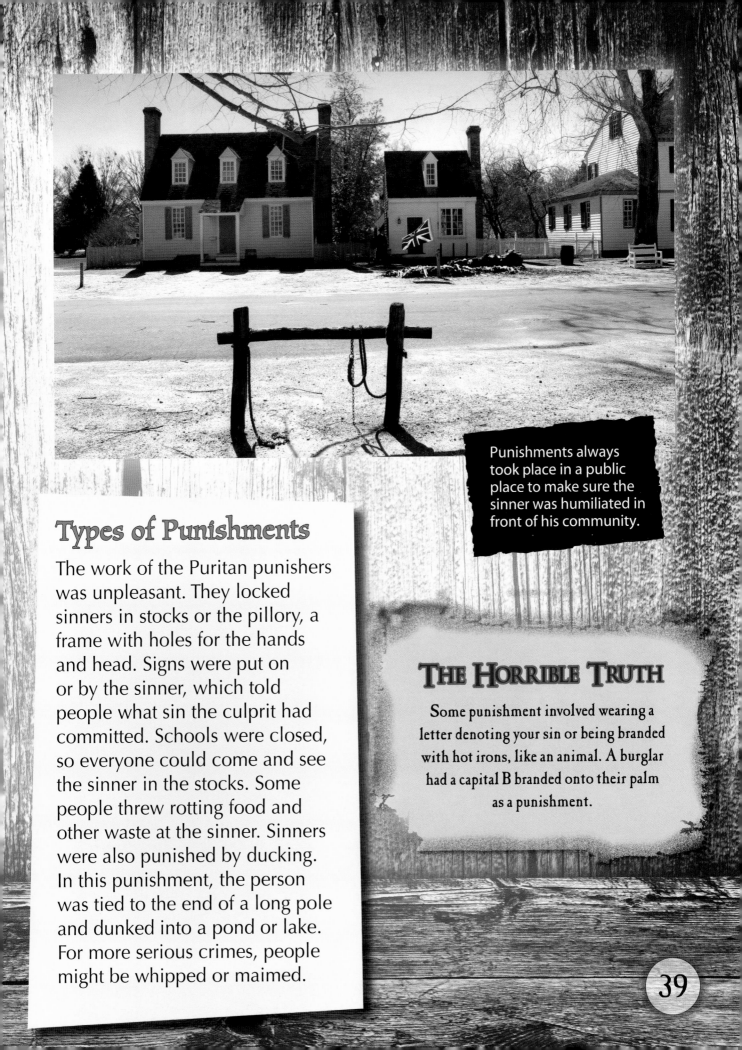

Punishments always took place in a public place to make sure the sinner was humiliated in front of his community.

Types of Punishments

The work of the Puritan punishers was unpleasant. They locked sinners in stocks or the pillory, a frame with holes for the hands and head. Signs were put on or by the sinner, which told people what sin the culprit had committed. Schools were closed, so everyone could come and see the sinner in the stocks. Some people threw rotting food and other waste at the sinner. Sinners were also punished by ducking. In this punishment, the person was tied to the end of a long pole and dunked into a pond or lake. For more serious crimes, people might be whipped or maimed.

THE HORRIBLE TRUTH

Some punishment involved wearing a letter denoting your sin or being branded with hot irons, like an animal. A burglar had a capital B branded onto their palm as a punishment.

Awful Apothecaries

If people are ill today, they go to a doctor for help. In colonial times, most people could only hope to see an apothecary, though the medical help they offered was limited.

In colonial times, sage was used as a medicine as well as in cooking.

The First Drugstores

There was a lot of sickness in colonial times and death rates from diseases, such as malaria, were high. Apothecaries prepared and sold medicines like a pharmacist does today. They often made remedies from herbs, animal parts, and other ingredients. Some natural remedies were successful, and some are still used today, such as chalk for heartburn, calamine for skin irritations, and cinchona bark for fevers.

Foxglove leaves were used as a medicine in colonial times.

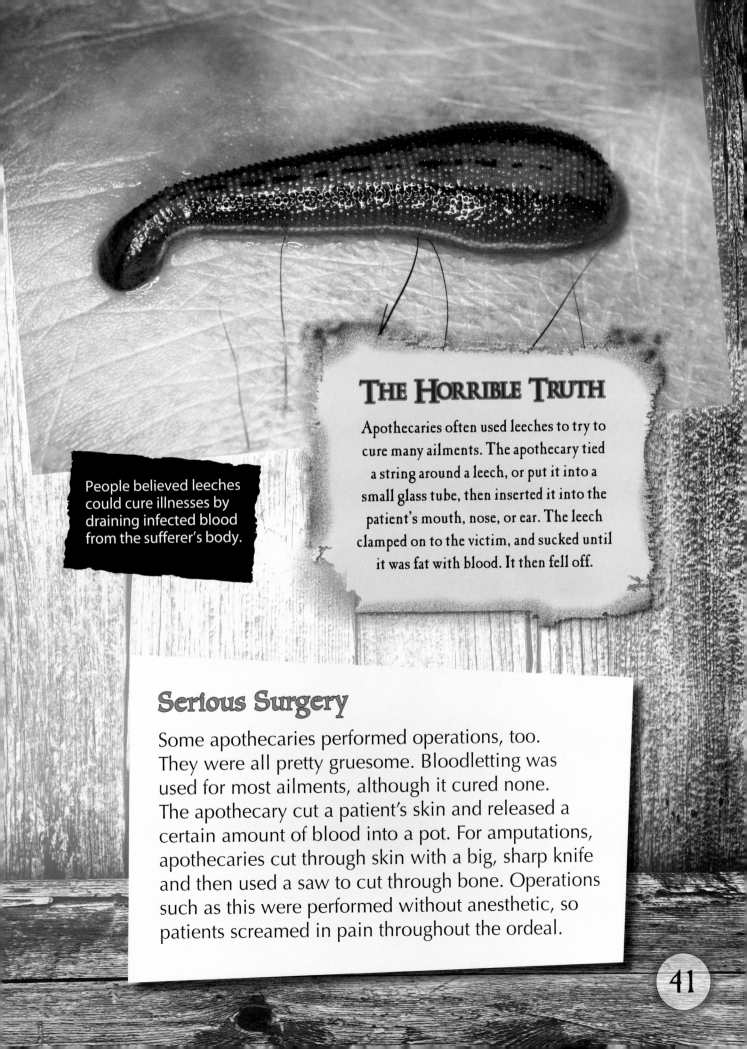

People believed leeches could cure illnesses by draining infected blood from the sufferer's body.

THE HORRIBLE TRUTH

Apothecaries often used leeches to try to cure many ailments. The apothecary tied a string around a leech, or put it into a small glass tube, then inserted it into the patient's mouth, nose, or ear. The leech clamped on to the victim, and sucked until it was fat with blood. It then fell off.

Serious Surgery

Some apothecaries performed operations, too. They were all pretty gruesome. Bloodletting was used for most ailments, although it cured none. The apothecary cut a patient's skin and released a certain amount of blood into a pot. For amputations, apothecaries cut through skin with a big, sharp knife and then used a saw to cut through bone. Operations such as this were performed without anesthetic, so patients screamed in pain throughout the ordeal.

Mad Hatters

In colonial times, almost everyone wore a hat when they left their homes. Women wore simple bonnets made from linen, cotton, or lace. They were worn to look respectable, but also to protect the wearer from the sun. Milliners made women's hats, and hatters made hats for men.

Women's hats, such as this bonnet, were often made of straw.

A Head for Style

A man's hat showed his social standing—and elaborate hats displayed a person's wealth. Colonial hatters made different types of hats, including the popular broad-brimmed hat or upturned brim, tricorne (three-cornered) hat. They made hats out of beaver skin, wool, cotton, or straw. Hats made of beaver felt that was brushed to shine like silk became very fashionable. Beaver fur was plentiful in the colonies, so the hat industry flourished.

The three-cornered "tricorne" hat was very popular with men during colonial times.

Mercury Madness

The mercury-induced madness that some hatters suffered later gave rise to the phrase "mad as a hatter."

Making Fur Hats

Beaver pelt was rough and greasy, so a hatter's first job was to remove the top layer of coarse hair with a knife or tweezers. Under this layer of hair was another layer of finer hairs. Hatters spread these hairs with a chemical solution that contained mercury. This helped to make a smooth felt. The fumes from the mercury were breathed in by the hatter, and they attacked the nervous system causing blurred vision, loss of balance, muscle twitching, and delusions.

Drops of mercury are highly toxic.

The End of Colonial Times

By 1770, more than 2 million people lived and worked in the North American colonies. The colonies had also become prosperous. Although each of the 13 colonies had its own local government, most decisions were still made in Britain. The colonists wanted to make these decisions themselves, so they rebelled against Britain.

The Revolutionary War

On April 18, 1775, British troops attempted to take a stock of weapons from colonists. However, a silversmith named Paul Revere had warned the colonial militia that the British were coming. The militia went to stop them. Shots were fired and the American Revolution began. The colonists organized their militias into an army under the command of General George Washington.

Colonial farmers, craftspeople, storekeepers, and laborers joined together to fight for the colonial militias.

Blacksmiths at War

The Revolutionary War was the American colonists' struggle for independence from British rule.

Colonial blacksmiths played an important role in the American Revolution. In secret, many blacksmiths made swords, knives, and horseshoes for the militias. They took a great risk—if caught by the British they could have been tried and hanged as traitors.

Declaration of Independence

On July 4, 1776, all 13 colonies declared themselves independent of Britain. The war continued until 1782, with the French, Dutch, and Spanish supporting the American colonists. Peace talks finally began in 1782, and were signed in 1783. The victorious Americans created a new nation made up of 13 states, which they named the United States of America.

Glossary

amputations surgical procedures in which part or all of a limb is removed

anesthetic a drug that stops a person feeling pain or puts them to sleep

anvil a heavy metal block with a flat top and a pointed end. Metal can be hammered and shaped on an anvil.

apprentice a person who learns a trade while working for an employer for low or no wages

attorney a lawyer

bridle headgear that a rider puts on a horse in order to handle it while riding

capsize to tip over a boat

career a job that a person does for a long time

charcoal burned wood

colony a piece of land under the control of another country

debt something, usually money, that one person owes another

delusions bizarre thoughts that have no basis in reality

export to send and sell goods or services to other countries

fermented broken down or turned sour

gangplank a plank used for getting on and off a boat or ship

gear wheel circular parts with teeth along the edges that interlock with and turn other gear wheels

harpoons long spears with hooked ends

hides animal skins

hubs the central parts of wheels

Industrial Revolution a period of rapid industrialization in Britain in the late eighteenth and nineteenth centuries

maimed wounded or injured

militia a group of civilians (nonsoldiers) trained as soldiers

milliners people who make or sell women's hats

nervous system the body system that includes the brain and nerves, which send messages from the sense organs (such as the eyes and nose) to the brain so a person can act on them

overseer a person who supervises or watches over others

pelts the skins of animals with the fur still on them

Pilgrims a group of English Puritans who sailed on the *Mayflower* and who founded the colony of Plymouth, Massachusetts, in 1620

plantations large estates on which export crops such as coffee, sugar, and tobacco are grown

rebellions fights against the authority of an organization or person

rigging a system of ropes, cables, or chains that supports a ship's masts and sails

self-sufficient able to grow and supply all your own food

sinful breaking one of God's laws or breaking a moral law

slaves people who are the legal property of other people and who are forced to obey the people who own them

synthetic artificial, man-made

vats large tanks or tubs

For More Information

Books

Benoit, Peter. *The British Colonies in North America*. New York, NY: Children's Press, 2013.

Hinman, Bonnie. *The Scoop on School and Work in Colonial America*. Mankato, MN: Capstone Press, 2012.

Raum, Elizabeth. *The Scoop on Clothes, Homes, and Daily Life in Colonial America*. Mankato, MN: Capstone Press, 2012.

Websites

Learn more facts about colonial and other eras in US history at:
usa.usembassy.de/history-colonial.htm

There are lots of pages about colonial jobs and daily life in Williamsburg at:
www.history.org/Almanack/life/trades/tradehdr.cfm

Discover interesting facts and pictures about colonial North Carolina at:
www.learnnc.org/lp/editions/nchist-colonial/6.0

Index